Youth In Sports

Females of Color

The dilemma in the Sports Industry with hiring Females of Color as Leaders. In K-12, Colleges and Universities.

How this problem is affecting female youth athletes that are of color

Copyright

"Never underestimate the power of dreams and the influence of the human spirit. We are all the same in this notion; the potential for greatness lives within each of us." -- Wilma Rudolph

ACKNOWLEDGEMENTS

I would like to say the adversity I experienced after college was more than I bargained for and for the first time, I truly underwent growing pains; which I felt to my core as a human being.

Up until this point, I had always landed on my feet, which was pretty high on the ladder. As an especially gifted basketball player, I worked hard, I studied hard, and I excelled at anything I set my mind to.

My chosen career paths did not go as planned, and I believed with everything in me they would. I was an adult and I had to do what adults do, taking the next best thing to earn a living for myself.

Was I a victim of being a female of color; aiming for positions that were in organizational climates and cultures which did not readily accept individuals who were different from their perceived notion of a co-worker, associate, team member or educator? I received all the necessary credentials including a Graduate D egree as well as being avery skilled athlete.

Once this realization occurred, I became true to myself in ways I never knew existed. I became comfortable in my own skin, while gaining the vision for my passion.

I was set to do all of these wonderful things I planned; not limiting myself to the corporate arenas, however as an author and entrepreneur sharing my knowledge, skills, and experiences. Including aiding in the building up of my community.

I have not looked back since my time in collegiate athletics, nor do I regret the adversity I endured.

I would like to thank my entire family for being such an intricate part of my life. Instilling in me a strong sense of family values and beliefs and pushing me to be the best version of myself.

Thank you, Dad, for stepping up to raise me, for giving me a loving, stable and disciplined home. For working two, three, or four jobs to support our family. The items and opportunities I thought were a part of growing up, realizing today that they indeed were extras - braces, cable, private schooling, vacations, and basketball year-round.

Also, to my Dad, thank you for keeping a ball in my hand, that ball allowed me to be everything I am today, so thank you for being my hero.

To my Mom, this adulting would have been in shambles without you stepping up, to redirect my thoughts and ideals. My Mother, indeed, is a special person, true to herself and truly one-of-a-kind. Without your persistence and determination these words would still be in my mind, not in this book.

To my second mother, Nicole; you have shown me what it means to be a lady and how to conduct myself as such. You, Nicole, became my stepmom by marrying my father, I believe you are an angel who came into my life at the most perfect time. Thank you for being that buffer between my Dad and I, while allowing me to be exactly who I am. I love you.

A special thanks to my forever best friend, my Grandma, Lueneal. Without her this would not be possible, I am her namesake, and she lives within me for forever.

FEMALES OF COLORS

My Grandmama, Oddie; the matriarch of the Ridley family, having over 150 descendants from you - family is nothing without you.

To my siblings, I say thank you for being who you are so that I can be me!

To JR, my forever fan, for teaching me to grow up so that I can be a role model for your children!

To Walter, my twin, for showing me how to be as cool as a cucumber and as observant as a saint!

To Marissa, for being my big sister, for showing me patience and honor.

To Selena and Andrew, my brother, sister cousins; thank you for checking on me when I was down and for telling me like it is.

To Shala, Nanyecma, Angela you will always be special to me, you are all my chosen sisters.

To all my relatives, both here and far away, thank you all for supporting me throughout my life choices and still keeping positive thoughts in your mind about me.

And to my partner, Lauren, whom I love very much, thank you for adding to my happiness and allowing me to add to yours.

Finally, to a host of wonderful friends, teachers, professors, coaches, mentors and community organizers and anyone else I would like to say thank you! I have been blessed with so much support during my life and I am now realizing just how precious my life has become because of it.

Chanell

Table of contents

INTRODUCTION

My name is Chanell Ridley and I decided to write this book to help Females of Color particularly among the *"Youth"* in the sports industry. As I continue to work with youths ranging in age from six to eighteen years of age, I still see the dilemmaI faced during my early years –

"Why Females of Color especially our Youth ask: What Perception of myself do I choose"

I am young, innocent, suggestible, vulnerable, and inexperienced. Are the people I listen to half of the time are they guiding me correctly and training me in the direction I should go?

I feel like l am being asked to conform to a new set of normalcy, a new culture and is it necessary for me to be in a sports program.

I have grown to love the sport so much; however, I do not want to be conditioned into being someone that I am not. My sports program takes up all my time, energy and devotion and my coaches go beyond instructing the rules of the game.

This dilemma needs to be brought to the light of day and positive suggestions given to resolve the issue.

I began my career in sports at the age of five and I continue even today, not directly playing but preparing girls between the ages of five to eighteen get ready if they so choose to enter the game either in school or as an extra-curricular activity.

I played in the following arenas throughout 20+ years:

1. 5 years of age to 10 years of age ---- Elementary School – After school

2. 10 years of age to 17 years of age ---- Summer AAU (Amateur Athletic Union)

3. 15 years of age to 18 years of age -----High School Varsity Team

4. 18 years of age -----State of Indiana All Star Team & Indiana North-South All Star

5. 18 years of age to 21 years of age------NCAA Division 1 University Women's Team

6. 21 years of age to 23 years of age------NAIA Division 2 University Women's Team

So, I know the topic of my book very well, I lived it every day of my life for over 20+ years.

I would like to share with females of color who love to play sports how to keep their perceptions of themselves strong, stable, unique, and true to what they believe and not what others may want them to believe or identify with. In this book we will touch on building a belief system, exclusive to who you are and your goals and dreams. However, a belief system that builds off your cultural identity that you were born into not a belief system that is foreign and feels artificial to who you truly are. What is your perception of yourself as a female of color in the sports industry?

I would additionally like to reveal to professionals in the sports industry the reality of this issue, so as they continue to look for harmony within their division, school, and teams. They realize the stark contrast in their players is due to cultural differences and not to push young impressionable youths in sports into thinking their belief system is wrong, because it is not the white stream of America's belief system.

Rather accept, each culture for the strengths it brings to the team. Performing different does not indicate the behavior is incorrect, belief systems dictate one's view of acceptable behavior. Who is to say a belief system is wrong or incorrect just because it is different? All belief systems that produce honorable qualities in an individual are all that matters. Are your perceptions based on a healthy mental and emotional state to work with impressionable youth in sports today from various cultures?

"People are only capable of operating at their level of understanding" – Susan Taylor

This book is based on my thesis I submitted for my graduate studies when I earned my Masters in Organizational Leadership. The information and data are very much relevant today and the problems still exist for Women of Color that choose to play sports.

I have added a "Problem / Solution" subchapter at the beginning of each chapter. It summarizes in everyday language some solutions that would help Females of Color that choose to play sports today.

Nonetheless, the academic research and facts are left intact for professionals who require literature reviews and studies to evaluate the underlined dilemma.

I am a very joyful and confident individual today and my perception of myself is very healthy, stable and I am very comfortable in my own skin.

I do what I love working with the youth population of my community and I am launching a strong business that will provide me financially while gaining generational wealth. It is my pleasure and my responsibility to help, especially because I know this issue still plagues our communities today. And no, I would not change any of my sports accomplishments, I love the game!

If there had been a book like this to read it would have helped me prepare for what I experienced.

Today this book is available!

FEMALES OF COLORS

CHAPTER I.

SPORTS & WOMEN OF COLOR

Subchapter

Problem & Solution

Problem

Females of color in leadership roles in the sports industry.

Females of color make up approximately 45% of the players in high school and college sports however, the leadership positions are mainly held by white men and women. Bringing with them their belief system and perceptions. Thereby setting the rules to match their viewpoint.

This is not done intentionally yet, without a diverse management team the possibility of the influence of the players will be geared toward a white mainstream culture.

This does not represent the nearly 45% of the players. Leaving such a misguided view for the players and mainstream media.

Solution

Athletic Departments should be required to undergo Diversity Awareness. Implement a strategic plan to diversify their department leadership and management to reflect the players on their teams.

Females of Color that participate in the sports industry must call their city councilmen, state representatives and federal representatives. Bring the issue to their attention and demand the same laws that require corporations, government entities and suppliers to meet diversity goals. This goal should have a deadline for athletic departments to fully put into place the needed changes. Eighteen months

This law needs to be implemented in the sports industry – the entire industry.

If 45% of your players are females of color, then your management/leadership needs to be 45% females of color.

As a result, cultural differences will not be an issue. The players can and will be understood by the leaders of their particular sport division.

Until the sports industry reflects the diversity in their leadership, females of color should find other mentors of color for Life Coaching.

<u>My Experience</u>

For me I did not see females of color in leadership roles as I played sports. What a difference this would have made for me during my playing years, it would have given me a deep sense of belonging.

CHAPTER I.

SPORTS & WOMEN OF COLOR

Women of color who have become successful through their sport are being called upon to be role models to young ladies. Femininity, athletic ability, heterosexuality, and social perceptions play huge roles in the scope of participating in sport as a young female of color.

These perceptions of youthful females of color, as studies state have negatively impacted how and what sports females of color participate in. The research conducted in this book focused on the missing element in the successfulness of females of color. With the inception of Title IX, more women have participated in sports. In recent years more females of color are actively participating in sports. Utilizing L. Harrison, Jr's Athletic Identity Measurement Scale (AIMS) questions were conducted to gather information of females of color's perception about sports. The information was derived from the athletes' perception of themselves and how others view them.

The surveyor conducted a series of questions directed at female athletes of color who actively participate in sports; the findings supported the linkage between personal success and success related to the sport.

The research conducted has shown the urgency for females of color to be in leadership roles, and how outsiders' perceptions influence decisions made by the young ladies. Through the conducted research, there were findings which represented the importance of positive media and societal perceptions of females of color whom have participated in sports.

CHAPTER II.

PERCEPTION – SPORTS ARE GREAT FOR FEMALES OF COLOR

Subchapter

Problem & Solution

<u>Problem</u>

Is the sports industry a good activity for females of color to enter while they are youths?

Playing sports is great for youths of any race and any age it builds up so many areas in their lives however, the stigma attached to females in sports as being "masculine" makes it difficult for many females of color to want to enter the field.

And those that do decide to play sports find it uneasy to accept many of the cultural differences that are thrust upon them as necessities to be a part of a team.

As a result, so many parents decide not to enroll their daughters in the sports industry. Leaving many females of color out of the possibilities of learning the fantastic benefits of discipline and responsibility skills that can be acquired and learned through participation on a sports team.

Females of color not playing as youth also miss out on the prospect of making the sports industry a career move. Not to mention the more females of color participate in sports as youths, this would allow females of color to acquire more leadership roles to level the playing field.

FEMALES OF COLORS

Solution

Leaders and the management team of each sports departments and their willingness to accept females of color with their cultural differences and not identify them with having behavior problems, because of the differences in cultural behavior.

More Education Boards requiring schools to actively enlist females of color as Coaches and Leaders in their sports departments. So, females of color during their youth can see the benefit to their lives overall.

Provide more information to parents on what playing sports can bring to their daughters coupled with the assurance there will be interaction with Leaders that are of color.

Colleges and Universities take an honest look at their Diversity and Inclusion within the Athletic Department.

More media attention showing a positive image of females of color playing on sports teams as youths highlighting the benefits.

My Experience

I loved playing sports from a noticeably young age, and I am grateful to have had the opportunity to play.

Other than the regular and nagging feeling of not belonging that I felt, this was a direct result of not seeing anyone who looked like me.

Playing sports gave me a sense of purpose, a reason to act responsible and it trained me to discipline myself. All great qualities the I still have today.

CHAPTER II.

PERCEPTION – SPORTS ARE GREAT FOR FEMALES OF COLOR

The idea behind sports in today's society is that sports provide positive outlets for all young people while teaching responsibility and the value of teamwork. The focus of this book is to gather information about youth in sports and the correlation between females of color in the arena of sports.

Females of color and sports play an important role in the shaping of the non-Caucasian community with additional opportunities for success than those who are not involved in sports. Female athletes of color can gain discipline while learning responsibility through their respective sport; this includes individual, team, and social responsibility. For some future athletes, participating in school athletics was their only opportunity to play a sport where the athletes could gain knowledge about responsibilities. The connection between sports and females of color for youth provides a constructive mechanism for staying out of trouble and having something to look forward to in the future.

Many females of color who actively participate in sports have overcome multiple obstacles within their own lives and respective households in order to compete in sports. Of those females of color whom are allowed to compete and engage in sports, they have sacrificed more than time or energy attaining their goals of playing sports. Those impediments include taking care of other family members in the household and working to provide for their families. As a student athlete, the ability to participate in sports can bring positive attributes to that individual, yet the idea of not helping their families financially can drain the young lady in ways which may not be filled again.

CHAPTER III.

PURPOSE OF SPORTS IN A SOCIETY

Subchapter

Problem & Solution

Problem

Sports have always been important to civilization and all cultures. The industry dates back to 2000 BC and brought with it many, many benefits. However, it only produces positive results when leadership accepts the team and directs with a full understanding of the team's strengths.

For the fan, sports are designed for entertaining for the society at large. We see someone we really like who can perform at the highest level, we flock to that individual or that sports team.

For many young people of color, they tend to follow, admire, and respect the athlete that directly represents who they are.

The fan has not been introduced to the operators behind the scenes of the game.

Solution

Remove the human bias from the sports industry and allow the games to reflect a society's greatness.

Allow all areas of the sports industry to be seen, felt, and heard.

We are aware that sports keep score for a reason, there is indeed a winner and a loser; however, the idea that I am participating at the highest level I can is an actual win.

There are many avenues for wins in the sports industry, not limited to scoring more points than your opponent. Representation matters, at each and every level and arena of sports.

My Experience

Playing sports allowed me to learn valuable lessons like leadership, setting goals and sportsmanship. It gave me additional educational benefits that my classes did not offer. I loved the game, so I was always willing to learn how to be an improved player.

CHAPTER III.

PURPOSE OF SPORTS IN A SOCIETY

Youth in sports is important to any society at large. The significance of sports in the African American community has been studied and researched, however females of color are being left behind. The purpose of this study was to link the constructiveness of participating in sports and females of color in any sport. There are numerous opportunities for females in sports today, for example Title IX.

Title IX was passed in 1972 requiring gender equality in sports for educational programs. The birth of Title IX has allowed females to participate in sports at the high school level as well as the collegiate level, since there has been an influx of females participating in sports. The correlation of the influx has granted more females of color the opportunity to participate in athletics than ever before.

This increases the ability to further their education based on the fact that they are an athlete. There are not enough publications on athletics and females of color, nor are there enough women who are speaking on the importance of sports in the communities of color.

'bas·ket·ball' (bas'kit-bôl'), n. 1. A game played by two opposing teams of five players each, on a rectangular court with a raised goal at either end, each team attempting to throw the ball through its own basket and to prevent the other team from scoring.

CHAPTER IV.

POTENTIAL SIGNIFICANCE

Subchapter

Problem & Solution

<u>Problem</u>

Females on the average have more issues with confidence and self-esteem. Some even suffer from depression. It is common in all races, and it affects females more often than their male counterparts.

If I am not as talented as those I see in the media; do I too have an opportunity to become a leader in athletics?

<u>Solution</u>

Females who play sports tend to have healthier lives, more self-confidence, and a positive self-image of themselves.

Realizing that playing sports is a team effort and that as long as I played the best game that my skills allowed me to play than I contributed to my team.

Having sports leaders who re-emphasize this point are such wonderful role models for youths to have in their lives, instead of just pushing to win at all costs.

FEMALES OF COLORS

We make our own mark, most of all the females of color who participate in a particular sport will not go professional. I must choose a path which pays me a livable wage while keeping me close to my sport of choice.

Examples include but are not limited to; Referee / Official, Athletic Departments, Coaching, Teaching, representation of other females of color in athletics.

<u>My Experience</u>

I was told all throughout my playing days that the opportunities for me to one day have a career as a sports leader was so within my reach. Well nevertheless, society had other perceptions of who they wanted astheir sports leaders.

CHAPTER IV.

POTENTIAL SIGNIFICANCE

A main goal for a young female of color whom has participated in sports could be to play their sports professionally. As a youthful athlete who has studied their sport while adhering to basic rules of self and others, the athlete could generate any goal and attain it. While participating in sports, the female of color will attend school regularly, be on time, and stray away from behavioral problems in order to compete in their sport. With guidelines in place for the female of color who participated in sports, there is more responsibility on the young lady, allowing her to rise to the occasion and become a leader.

Guidelines within a school setting were followed by student athletes due to the importance of participating in their sport. The young ladies were more respectful to teachers and staff members as well as their peers, leading by example. Coaches were viewed as mentors to the young ladies in their particular sport and in their personal lives too. The constructive and motivational improvements made in the lives of the young ladies poured down on the athletes from their coaches, which allowed for the females of color to reach personal goals.

The significance of talking about sports in communities of color with females can heighten the awareness of where athletics can take an athlete in her life. Using other females of color to mentor youth will be beneficial to all people within that community. For females who participate in sport, the opportunity to receive a scholarship to attend college may be the only chance these females have to continue their education. When society tunes into sports through the media, people may see an abundance of athletes who are of color. Athletes who set out to make a career out of their respective sport in college have a higher chance to play professionally.

25

CHAPTER V.

SUCCESS

Subchapter

Problem & Solution

Problem

What is success for me?

Most often youth in sports identify success based on outcome of what they are participating in. Success tends to mean scoring points or goals. Winning the game.

Females of color that play sports during their youth normally consider a college scholarship or being able to play sports professionally as the ultimate success story.

Solution

The only actual thing that matters is improving oneself, and not trying to be like others. Many youth in sports base our own success on what others have done.

Yet, it is all about how you perceive and prepare. If you prepared well, the outcome really does not matter. The hard work and preparation will pay off in the long run.

Having people in your life who are supporting you and are there to help you in your journey along the way. Keep people that bring positivity in your life around, because not only will they encourage you, but they will also help lift you up when you need it most.

"Success is peace of mind, which is a direct result of self-satisfaction that comes from knowing you did your best to become the best you that you are capable of becoming." – John Wooden

My Experience

Throughout my sports career it appeared to me that if we as females of color are still in a school environment then our success in the sports industry is allowable and acceptable.

However, it is as adults striving for a career position in sports that we run into society's obstacle or the preconceived assumption that is woven in the sports industry.

That somehow females of color are not good candidates for leadership positions no matter what their background.

Is it that they are unaware this is their preconceived culture or is it deliberate?

CHAPTER V.

SUCCESS

How are these athletes successful and where did it all start? This idea that an athlete must be the best to be successful is derived from the media. Utilizing the sport athletes participate in to reach another goal is equally as important as professional athletes are. Although there are many females' athletes who do not participate in sports professionally, they are still able to share their love of the sport through different careers.

Questions

These questions were asked and answered through the survey which was given to participants.

1. Are females of color more likely to succeed if they participate in sports?

2. Is the criterion or standard for females of color who participate in sports harder than white females?

3. What is the importance of utilizing females of color who have already participated in sports to return to tell their success story?

4. How does one measure athletic success?

5. Who measures success for female athletes of color?

Limitations

This study did not focus on all athletes, it just looked at the significance of females of color participating in sports and how the athlete's community can benefit from the success of the females. The focus was on females of color, adolescents who are actively participating in sports, and their perception of what their sport can do for them. The research did not include specific communities of color who do not participate in sports.

CHAPTER VI.

THE PUBLIC REVIEW

Subchapter

Problem & Solution

Problem

There does not appear to be enough females of color in historically black communities that play sports or have positions of success in sports to filter down to the youth in communities of color.

Society at large and the media portray a negative overall image of females of color that play sports. There are only a few athletics that have a positive image generally.

The sports industry has got to see the problem for what it is and correct it by actively hiring females of color in leadership rolls from K-12 to the professional settings.

Solution

More females of color that have played sports for years and understand the dilemma should step up and give back to their communities in a way that gives a positive representation for the youth.

Media coming on board to highlight the encouraging stories that are happening across the country that involves all females of color whether youth or adults.

Parents striving to encourage their daughters to enter the sports field if there is a desire and have the willingness to provide the support, guidance, and resources for young females to participate throughout their K-12 school years.

If the sports industry is not willing to change within its own ranks, then society must force the change by everyone bringing attention to the truth of the problem. Including Government intervention.

My Experience

I feel compelled to speak out and step up to share my experiences, my views, and some truths for females of color in the sports industry.

I will continue to help female athletes that are of color at any age by being a mentor and giving of myself in areas that are lacking in the sports leadership currently. A point of view from a different culture adding to the diversity of the industry itself.

Cultural diversity is displayed on the field of so many sports games by the variety of races. Leadership has to catch up to exhibit the same.

CHAPTER VI.

THE PUBLIC REVIEW

Throughout the literature review, the findings have been focused on the ability for women to compete in their respective sport while maintaining their femininity and striving toward their personal goals attaining to success. Mean and Kassing state, "We seek in this work to move beyond mere indications of participation in sport by women, to better understand how female athletes construct their sporting identities and the degree to which these constructions reflect traditional male hegemony or substantive changes within the community of sport" (Mean & Kassing, 2008, p.127).

Females of color who participate in sports are subjected to stereotypes from all areas surrounding their sport (Duke & Greer, 2008). McVee, Dunsmore & Gavelek, (2005) state "Gender schema suggest that individuals learn the differences between the classification of male and female from society and then adjust their behaviors to meet those expectations" (p. 534). Society forms expectations of individuals and situational outcomes through stereotypes and norms, and if the norms do not come, individuals can become uneasy (Jones & Greer, 2011). Individuals generate assumptions and logical expectations through society developing specific behaviors of schema. Often activities are geared and learned as children towards gender appropriate roles, according to society's views (Jones & Greer, 2011). Athletes have been portrayed as participating in a sport which is applicable to how their appearance and stature is perceived (Duke & Greer, 2008).

Female athletes of color have been sex-typed by the media (Hardin & Greer, 2008). Jones and Greer stated, "Another common stereotype in sport is that women are not credible athletes" (p. 359). "Title IX of the Educational

Amendment Act of 1972 mandated equal opportunity for women in educational institutions receiving federal funding, and effectively increased competitive female athletic participation in the United States" (Holschen, 2004, p. 852). This was the beginning of inter-collegiate athletics for women, allowing them to participate and earn scholarships in their respective sport, thus creating a movement for all females to actively compete towards a career in sports. Female student athletes of color face multiple challenges when entering the realm of sport, including sexism, racism, and heterosexuality. "Indeed, rather than reducing female stereotyping, the increase in women's sporting presence has worked to raise awareness and concern about female athletes' sexuality and thus the need to negotiate discourses of traditional beauty, size, and femininity" (Caudwell, 1999; Mean & Kassing, 2008, p. 127).

Female student athletes of color spend copious amounts of hours perfecting their specific skills related to their particular sport, combined with the problems these females face pertaining to their ability. "To be devoid of the traditional markers of femininity are to be in an unnatural body, and this unnaturalness is most often associated with homosexuality" (Veri, 1999, p. 356).

Natural identity must be congruent with society and media's perception of female athletes. Quietness and docility no longer represent the primary markers for signifying normative girlhood (Adams, Schmitke & Franklin, 2005). Through the influx of more females participating in sports, their femininity is in question the harder those young ladies compete. Adams, et al. (2005) expresses the power of heteronomativity of sports, to be a good athlete is to be gay.

The idea of preserving femininity to female athletes is nothing new. By the 1930s, the image of promiscuity as an athlete had changed to that of a mannish, lesbian athlete (Cahn, 1993). This image turned away heterosexual women in the 1950s – at the same time sports provided a safe haven for lesbians and questioning women (Cahn, 1994). Pat Griffin states "This high promotion of sexualized and highly heterosexualized image has become even more explicit today" (Griffin, 1992, p. 261). Person et al. states, "Although scholarships allow the institution to attract high-quality athletes, this does not guarantee that the athletes will graduate" (Person, Benson-Quaziena & Rogers, 2001, p. 59).

Many female athletes of color enter college unable to keep up with the academic pressures involving being eligible and graduating. Many females of color entering college identify themselves in respect to their individual sport, thus embracing every aspect of that sport the athletes have seen, read about, heard, and lived until this point. Mean and Kassing state, "Nonetheless, women have increasingly entered the sporting arena, working to achieve athletic inclusion and, hence, identities" (Mean & Kassing, 2008, p. 129).

Essays by Experts Researchers who have studied the effects of Title IX in regard to females of color in sport have found that the ability to adapt into becoming a successful student-athlete and positive role model are lost without feedback and mentoring from female athletes of color who have experienced the struggle.

According to Comeaux (2010), the following major themes exude females of color in sports: (1) success in spite of sport demands, (2) color-blind ideology, (3) success in spite of race, and (4) racially coded language. Life experiences mold and shape how people live their lives. Female athletes of color are at a disadvantage of succeeding academically according to the review of the literature. Comeaux (2010) examines the relationship between success rates in graduating college and faculty perceptions of female athletes of color.

There is an obvious lack of females of color in positions of power, such as faculty members of colleges. The lack of culturally competent individuals in faculty positions show a lack of interest in these positions along with negative perceptions of how to succeed in collegiate decision-making skills when entering their respective sport.

There are not enough females of color in positions of success to filter down to the youth in communities of color. Positive images of female athletes of color within communities provide discourse for female athletes to strive to be like the role models they see every season. The media has portrayed female athletes of color as positive role models, with women's basketball leading the pack as it is the premier sport for females. Female athletes participating in sports studies have shown an overwhelming support of sexism derived from the media's portrayal of a feminine athlete (Adams et al., 2005).

Research states socialization as a process and how female African American youth experience it affects the likelihood of them becoming involved in sports and which sport, they have chosen (Bruening, Pastore & Armstrong, 2008). The socialization into sports for females of color is different historically from the experience of Anglo women (Smith, 1992). For African American women who have participated in sports, the social order has included the labeling of the sports which are desirable for them to play (Bruening et al., 2008). These social expectations contribute to a socialization process that leads most women of color to participate in basketball and track and field. In examining the socialization of African American females, then, it is crucial to look at people who influence their sport (Bruening et, al, 2008).

Related Research Seeking to promote a psychological sense of community has been a focus for colleges to their students (Berryhill & Bee, 2007). Involvement in campus activities, living arrangements and class rank are all entered into the psychological sense of community for students. Many studies have focused on student traits connected to senses of community, yet a limited characteristic is ethnicity (Berryhill & Bee, 2007). The racial climate including student perceptions of racial tension, ethnic discrimination and relations among members of other ethnic groups factor into how these students adjust to campus life (Hurtado, Millem, Clayton-Pedersen & Allen, 1998).

Maximizing athletes' success is varied from sport to academics to personal life; females of color who have participated in sport embody a specific contemporary model of womanhood, however they sacrifice autonomy in the process (Foster, 2003). Female athletes of color were being treated by assumptions from the athletic department based on racialized expectations of behavior (Foster, 2003). This has created a dependency on the athletic department for structure and guidance to the females of color participating in sports.

Females of color were taught to rely on the athletic department for class scheduling, tutoring, academic advising and personal and professional development (Foster, 2003). Webster's Dictionary defines panoptic as "A prison so constructed that the inspector can see each of the individuals at all times without being seen, all things are visible" (Webster's Dictionary, 2011). This definition exemplifies the structure to which these young ladies are spending their time. This will cut back on outside interference for females of color who have been predisposed due to their sport of choice.

Specific time frames and block scheduling around practice and competitions allow for a strict, detailed-oriented path to success. Athletes are viewed as role models, from their peers to how they are portrayed in the media (Foster, 2003). Utilizing specific coaches and creating positions of leadership for females of color generates assumptions of how to deal with a certain group of athletes. The athletic department has been responsible for protecting vulnerable females of color (Foster, 2003). Feminism, as it has historically has been positioned, has often been made more reverent to Anglo women (Collins, 1991). Possible factors influencing students' attitudes about feminism, or likelihood of self-identifying as a feminist, are negative in regards to sexual harassment, sex discrimination or gender violence (Winkle-Wagner, 2008).

What is needed is not for more women to self-identify as a feminist, but a new adaptation of gender roles without perpetuating gender stereotypes encouraging innate strength as females of color in sports (Winkle-Wagner, 2008). Research has pointed in the direction of exploiting athletes of color, without room for career opportunities after their sport (Meggysey, 2000).

Athletes have less time available for the educational process that extends beyond going to class every day to socializing with research groups (Hawkins, 1999). Due to psychological and physical fatigue from participation in sports, student athletes have decreased levels of motivation to study (Beamon & Bell, 2002; Person, Benson-Quaziena & Rogers, 2001). Through social expectations of gender, race/ethnicity and class, there have been successful women of color in sports organization (Smith, 1992).

Research states that women of color have been socialized to work, yet most do not achieve high-ranking professional positions (Higgenbotham, 1992; Smith, 1992). Striving towards success allows for ground-breaking while promoting personal strength, character, and achievement goals as a female of color. Within the African American community, traditional achievements have been a source of pride for the youths. Rich traditions of family extend in the African American communities; setting high standards for the young people to succeed (Smith, 2005).

Concordia Lutheran High School
This certifies that
Chanell Ridley
has been awarded the VARSITY LETTER
in
Varsity Girls Basketball
for the season of 2002-03
Coach
Athletic Director
You have to EXPECT THINGS of
yourself before you can do them.
Michael Jordan
Cadets
C

CHAPTER VII.

SURVEYS OF FEMALE ATHLETES OF COLOR

Subchapter

Summary

It is so important to gain an overall view from actual sports players that are of color and female.

It gives a clear picture of how most females from communities of color feel, think and perceive themselves and the overall sports industry from where they sit.

We know people are only capable of operating at their level of understanding yet, the participants in my study gave their view, their perception, their truth.

Imagine if there were females of color leaders in the sports arena that truly represented the percentage of females of color players.

The number of participants I attempted to reach would have increased substantially.

The answers would have reflected the true meaning of sports in a healthy society.

So many females of color would be benefiting from what playing sports has to offer.

So many lives could advance.

The sports industry has to see the value!

CHAPTER VII.

SURVEYS OF FEMALE ATHLETES OF COLOR

Overall Approach and Rationale With the surveys, the concept was to understand how female athletes of color view their athletic status and the importance of their individual sport. The survey used (see Appendix A), Questionnaire 1 was a previously used instrument, yet not all three had been used together.

The first survey asked questions concerning the athletic appearance and depth of the female athlete of color's respective sport. These specific questions (Q1-Q10) were asked to understand the athlete's viewpoint of sports. This instrument was derived from L. Harrison, Jr. (et al.), Athletic Identity Measurement Scale (AIMS) (Harrison, 2011). The survey contained three separate instruments which were asked in different times to generate critical answers of self-perception. Additionally, the first set of questions asked questions about self as an athlete and how closely related sports are to these females of color who participated in the survey.

The second section of the survey was developed to comprehend how females of color chose their sport and if success is tied in with their sport of choice. This survey was ten questions (Q1-Q10) asked in succession with Part 1; at a later time. These questions were asked to generate the true meaning of being successful for these females of color with educational undertones. This survey pushed the females to think about their current position with their sport and how competitive they were as an athlete.

There was a key used (see Appendix A, Part II), numbers one through seven, with one being 'Never' and seven being 'Always'. These questions were asked to females of color with perceptions of their respective sport and how they were viewed. The final section of the survey instrument (see Appendix A, Part III) was incorporated to capture the demographics of the respondents. As stated in the topic and overall section, only females of color were surveyed on their perceptions of sport and other's perception of the athletes in a particular sport. Age, educational level, ethnicity, and sport were identified in this instrument. Age ranged from 11-25 to capture female youth who participated in sports, attempting to look at these perceptions through different maturity levels (although this survey instrument was not longitudinal).

Furthermore, the survey instrument did not inquire about the length of time participated in any specific sport, for the data collected was used for immediate information gathering and not over a period of time for any particular female of color.

Site Population Selection

The focus was to gather age-appropriate females of color who were athletes and how these young ladies viewed themselves. The criteria for participants included:

1) Female / With Ethnic decent

2) Enrolled in School (Elementary through College-aged subjects)

3) Females who actively participated in sports (of any kind)

4) No females of color who participated in sports with the author or during the same time frame as the author (At Miami University or University of Saint Francis – within the last five years)

Females who are not of color were not the targeted subjects for this particular survey instrument. As stated in the introduction, this book had a focal point on young ladies of color. With females who participate in sports outside of an organized league, their perceptions are different for various reasons; their answers might have caused outliers in the conclusions. Specific subjects were gathered through outreach of the author to mentors, coaches, teachers, and parents for females of color to participate in the survey. Environmental factors were accounted for, and limitations were taken into consideration.

Subjects invited to participate in the research survey included young ladies involved with sports on a competitive level while attending school. The area in which the author used to gather participants included Fort Wayne, IN and Allen County, community organizations such as The Fort Wayne Greater YMCA, Fort Wayne Community Schools (FWCS), East Allen Community Schools (EACA), peers and various associates of the author. Data Gathering Methods This survey was delivered to various individuals in positions of leadership with the females of color; either as a mentor or coach the completed survey was then collected.

During the spring of 2013, the surveys were completed and returned to the author for data collection and analysis. The young ladies selected for the survey were screened with ability from the author on ethnicity and educational level (in order to comprehend the questions). Fifty females of color were asked to participate in the survey; twenty-five females completed the survey. Data Analysis Procedures After fourteen days of participant selection, conducting surveys and collecting the completed questions, the results were transferred to extract the data.

Part I of the survey was scored with 'Strongly Disagree' as 1 to 'Strongly Agree' as 4, resulting in higher scores for the participants. This showed the females how sport influenced their life. The author wanted to gather how females of color honestly viewed their participation in sports. The summative score was 40 (Strongly Agree for Q1- Q10) and the median was 20. There were no correspondents who responded negatively (strongly disagree) to Q1, 'I consider myself an athlete'. All members who participated in the survey were considered (perceived) to be competitive athletes and thus subgroups were not derived from the surveys. Of the twenty-five participants, all considered themselves athletes and understood how their sport was perceived by others and the media. Perceptions of the female as an athlete of self, and how others view their sport ability can affect the sport the young lady will choose, and their comfortability with that sport.

Table 1- Perceptions of Female athletes of color

	High	Moderate	Low
(Self) Positive Perceptions	>30	15-30	<15
(Self) Negative Perceptions	<15	15-30	>30
(Others) Positive Perceptions	>30	15-30	<15
(Others) Negative Perceptions	<15	15-30	>30

Part II of the survey asked to connect success from sports-oriented goals and team-oriented goals for success of that particular sport. These questions were asked to signify how young females of color perceived themselves in the sport they participated in. Furthermore, the data was gathered to possibly correlate females to play sports due to similar connections with other women who have participated in their sport choice. Participants who scored about a 30 were perceived as 'true' athletes; in that these females of color loved to participate in their sport. To those females of color who participated in the survey, their life revolved around sports, and the success of that particular sport.

Of those individuals whom scored between 15 and 30, they were considered athletes; however, their life does not depend on the success of their sport. These females have goals and desires outside of sport and how it has related to their personal success.

Respondents who scored under 15 were not viewed as 'true' athletes because their personal and sport-oriented goals are not connected. For these young ladies who scored below 15, winning and accolades were not a focal point for their individual success. Part III of the survey examined the demographics as it pertained to sport, ethnicity, education, and age.

The preconceived notion of particular females to participate in specific sports was something that would not be considered in the data collection. Certain females of color who participated in varied sports had different levels of conformity within their sport. Each sport represented different perceptions of their particular sport from self and others.

Trustworthiness

The questions were asked in an effort of the author to generate critical thinking of self as it pertained to their sport. Most of the questions were asked and may have generated the same response, yet with different perceptions. The data was hand collected, and the respondents did not meet the author, however the participants did know who the author was.

The participants were asked to be anonymous with their completion of the survey; however, some identified themselves (those completed instruments were not used in compliance with anonymity of the data collected).

Ethical Consideration Informed consent was given by the surveyed participants prior to completion of the survey. As stated earlier, data was not collected from participants who identified themselves. This survey did not conflict with any incentives for the author or participants involved.

CHAPTER VIII.

FINDINGS

Subchapter

Summary

The finding of my survey's reflects the dilemma in most communities of color in today's society, the younger the participant the more desire and belief that there is.

If I work hard enough, follow all the rules, and get good grades in school, I can achieve the *"American Dream"* even in the sports industry.

However, as the participants get older the reality of seeing females of color who contributed to the game with everything, they had to give including having skills for the game. Older participants notice that these females of color were not fully accepted into the industry as adult leaders in career positions within the sports arena.

The assumption they have is "why should I pursue sports; it is not a business or trade that accepts persons of color no matter how great your skills are or what you have to offer to the players. It requires so much investment with little or no return as a professional career choice".

We have an obligation to the future generations that have the desire and the love of the game to level the playing field.

Sports leaders need to reflect the players. Decision makers, coaches, and officials.

The time has come to reveal the truth of this problem in our society!

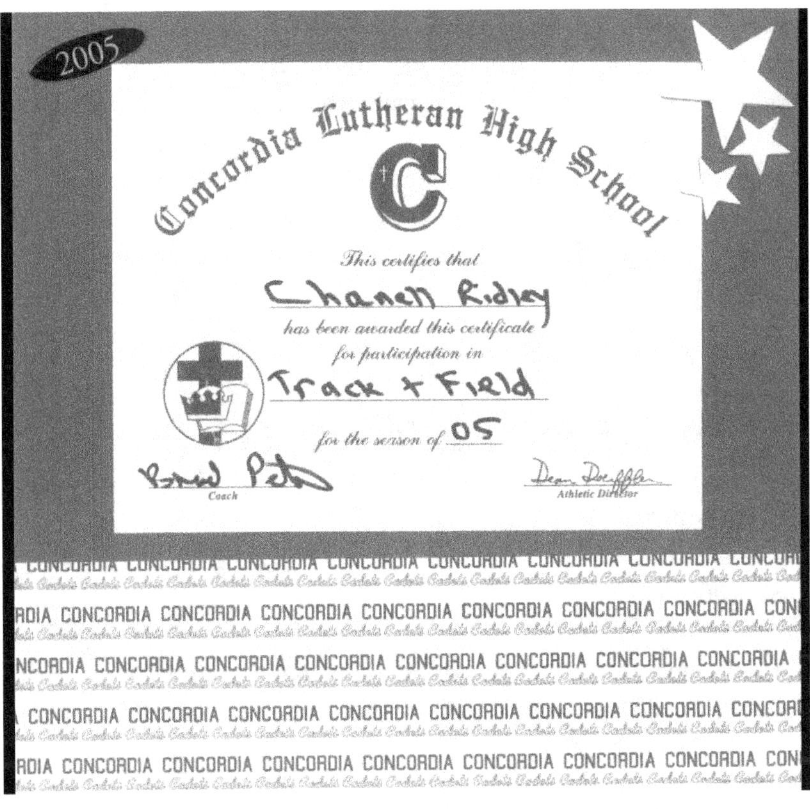

CHAPTER VIII.

FINDINGS

Findings: The following graphs display that the respondents of this study wereyoung ladies who are beginning their athletic career up to college graduates with varying levels of sport participation. Many of the respondents were under the age of eighteen, with parental/guardian consent to participate; concluding that these youthful athletes were not high school graduates. The respondents were from multiple ethnic backgrounds, with the highest in African-American females. Furthermore, only females were invited to join in the study and also the focus was to generate perceptions of females of color who participate in sports.

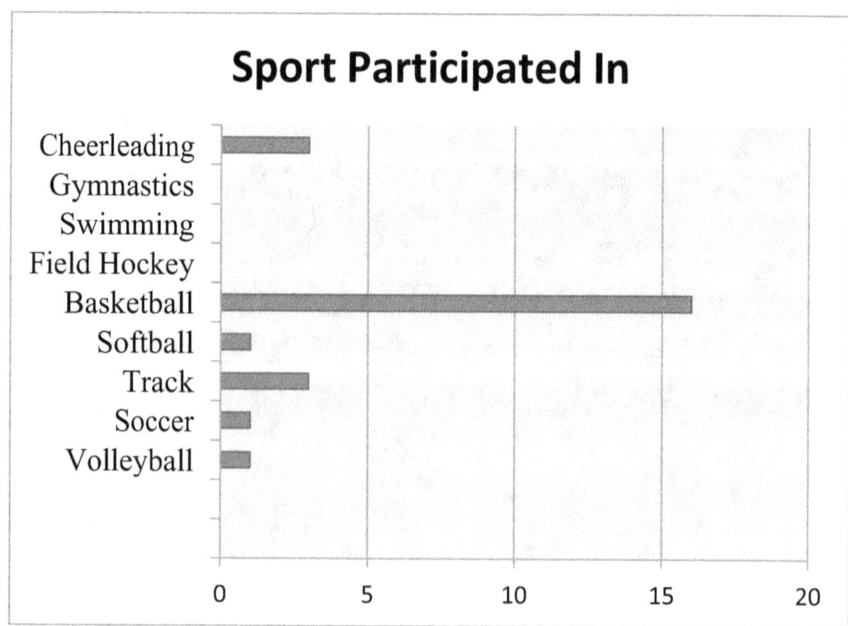

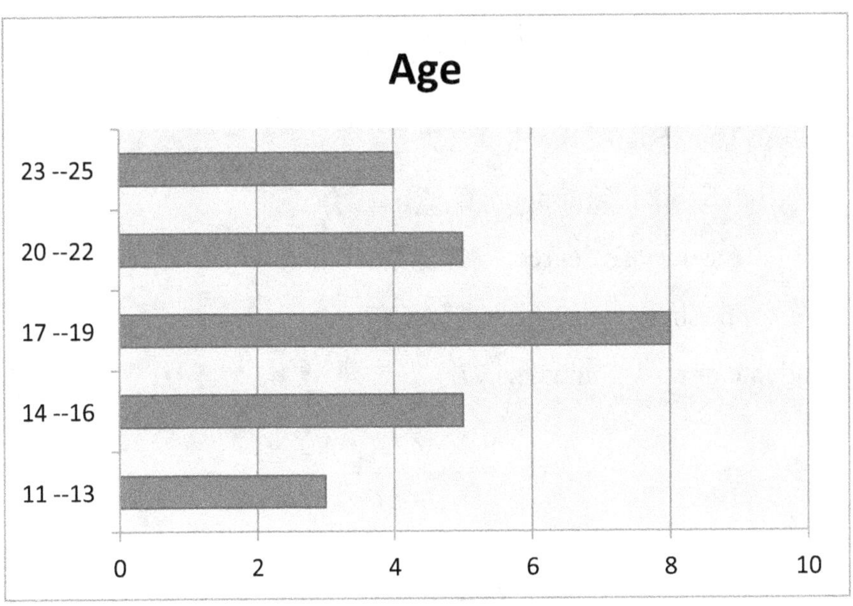

Age
23 --25
20 --22
17 --19
14 --16
11 --13
0
2
4
6
8
10

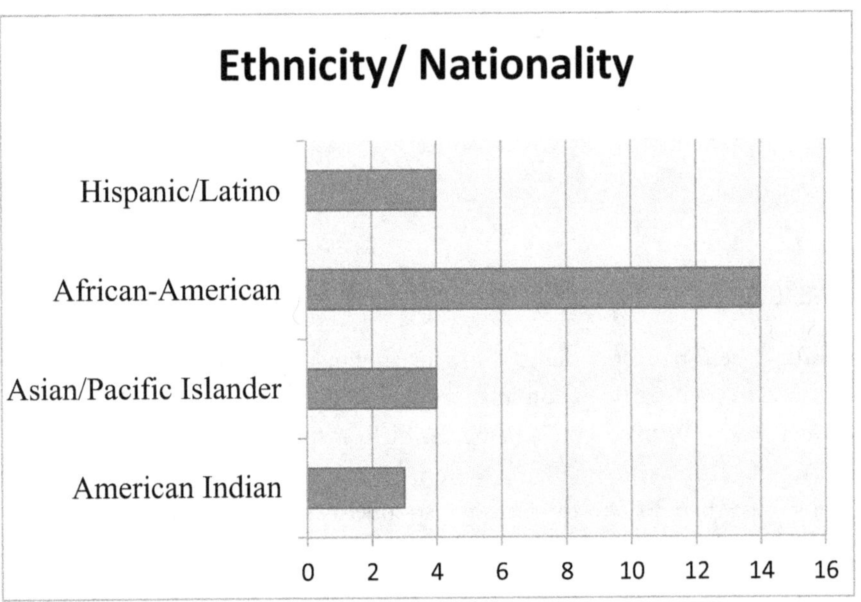

Ethnicity/ Nationality
Hispanic/Latino
African-American
Asian/Pacific Islander
American Indian
0
2
4
6
8
10
12
14
16

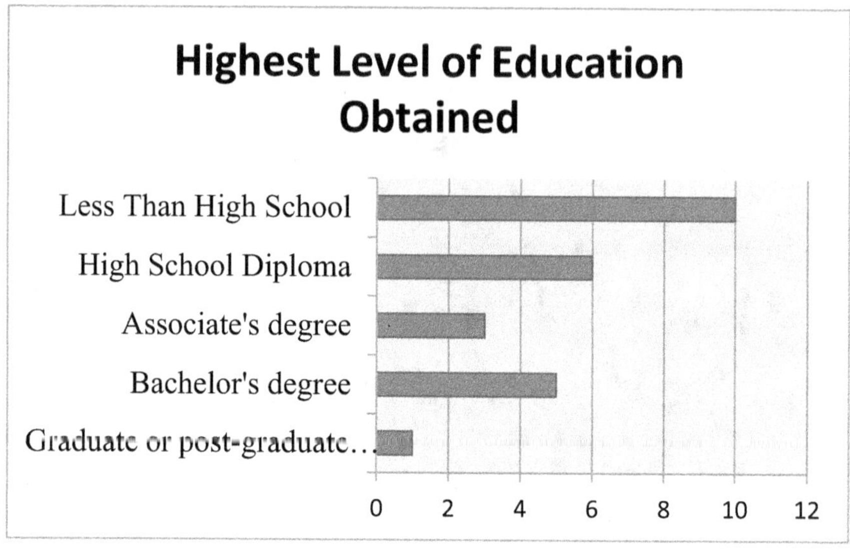

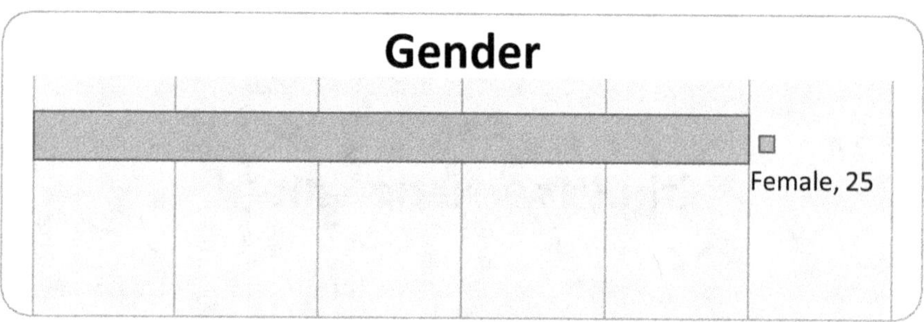

Participants: Perceived view of sport on self as an athlete.

Result: True. The respondents who scored high on their view of self as it pertained to their participation in sport viewed themselves as a leader and so did their peers. With seven (7) being the highest score of 'always,' while the lowest was 'never' with a one (1), there were many high scores with the results. Less than 30% of the female respondents scored low on how their sport is identified through themselves.

FEMALES OF COLORS

One particular question asked on the questionnaire, "I am in school because of my sport, and without it I would not be in school" scored high with many respondents concluding a striving for success through society's viewpoint. Of the participants, all 15 of the collegiate-aged and high school graduates answered with a five (5) or higher.

There is a definite correlation between how the young ladies view themselves and also how they perceive others to view them. There were many females of color who scored high on the question of their success in regards to their sport. The linkage of the successfulness of the sport as it pertains to the female of color has been engrained through media perceptions from that particular sport.

Table 2 – Self-perceptions of value and success

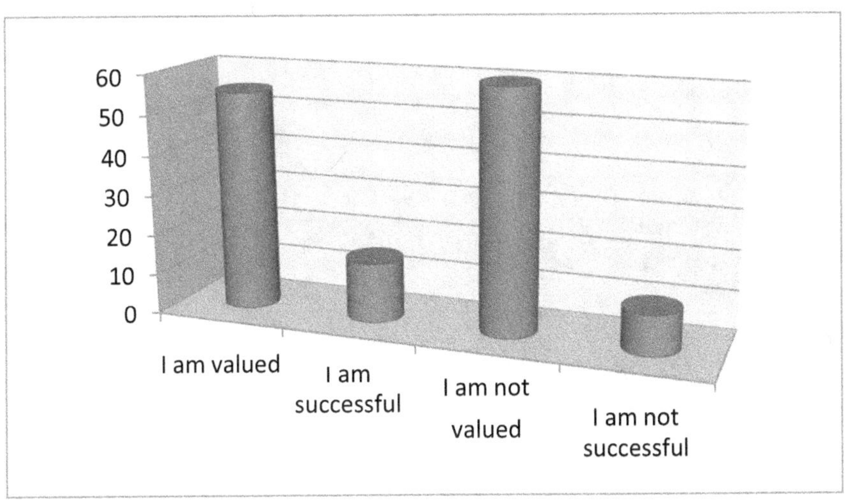

Participants: Other people see me as an athlete.

Result: True. The perceptions of others involved with these females of color mainly see the young ladies as athletes; nearly 75% of the respondents thought other's viewpoint was of an athlete. All of the females were alone taking the survey, however many of the participants were involved in sports because of other people encouraging their participation. With that being said, many of the respondents were in the process of being conditioned to do well in their sport by coaches, parents, mentors and also peers; placing pressure on the success of self. There were many females who were aware of specific perceptions when participating in their sport; this did cause a correlation of others' perceptions along with self-perceptions.

Table 3- Life goals related to sport / Importance of sport

	Strongly Disagree	Disagree	Agree	Strongly Agree
I need to participate in my sport	8	2	12	3
My goals are sport related	2	3	5	15
Sports are most important to me	5	2	10	8
Sports are my Only importance	6	4	7	8
I am depressed if injured and cannot participate	5	3	8	9

Participants: Younger correspondents viewed their life goals with their sport related goals.

Result: True. The participants aged eleven to fifteen placed more emphasison succeeding in their sport due to the pressured of society and their respective nationality. Many adolescents are easily swayed by their peers and what others think about those young ladies. Specific questions were generated to help the females of color actively think about how their sport has impacted their lives. Competitively as a young female of color, there are expectations placed on the athlete by the media encouraging the success of the athlete because of their perceived athletic ability.

In comparison, Appendix A (Questionnaire II) describes the differences in age, from eleven to twenty-five. As a young adult, these females are portrayed by the media as highly stereotyped, and their success relies on their athletic ability. As an athlete of color, to be involved with athletics at a high intensity level of competition is to open oneself up to society's views on how the young lady conducts herself.

VOLUME 2, ISSUE 1 • NOVEMBER 18 – DECEMBER 1, 2005 • VISIT US ONLINE AT WWW.NEIGAMENIGHT.COM
PT-15
NORTHEAST INDIANA GAMENIGHT
GIRLS PRESEASON
TOP 15 TEAM
THE STARTING FIVE
These five players highlight Northeast Indiana GameNight's Preseason Top 15 team.
Kara Boester
DeKalb
Senior • Guard
Sha'la Jackson
South Side
Junior • Guard
Mackenzie Warwick
Norwell
Senior • Guard
Chanell Ridley
Concordia
Senior • Forward
Danielle Ben-Tsvulun
Harding
Senior • Forward

CHAPTER IX.

CONCLUSIONS

Subchapter

Summary

The Sports Industry has to see the Value in Change!

Everyone in our Country, in our Society, in our Communities appreciates watching and contributing to Sports!

Concordia Lutheran High School Congratulates
CHANELL RIDLEY
2006 INDIANA ALL-STAR
GOOD LUCK AT MIAMI OF OHIO!

CHAPTER IX.

CONCLUSIONS

Conclusions: The similarities with the results of the surveys conducted with respect to the researcher included success conjoined with the success of the individual within their sport. Young ladies who competed in sports were more likely to help other females of color in a role model format, without understanding what a leader consists of.

Perceptions of self for those females of color included internal struggles which stemmed from their lifestyle, and which sport they participated in. The researcher stated the societal perceptions of female athletes; this included the heterosexual and mannish overtones of sports in general. Many females have not been identified as athletes by the public, causing a push for those young women to act a specific way to receive a specific reaction.

As a result of the demographic consisting of all minority ethnicities, the standard of the society is that those who are not Caucasian are struggling more than others. With that being said, this was not a focal point of the researcher's study when it came to the success of females of color participating in sports. In the world of competition as it has pertained to sports, minorities were and are viewed as the majority.

Solving the problem of females of color in sports, there have been leadership gaps to create a lineage of respect for minority athletes. The leader must possess knowledge of community and also an understanding of sports with the combination of success to athletes. As it pertained to the success of younger athletes (ages eleven through fifteen), there was a correlation with success in their sport and success in their life. The researcher concluded that the correlation was most likely due to the push to be independent as a female of color.

Another conclusion which related to younger females was that there were not enough positive leaders in their current sport. In summary, participation in sports for a young female of color has resulted in an increase of self-esteem, leadership skills, team building, and, most importantly, the joys of success through work ethic. The measuring of success is determined by the individual, the meaning of success has been interpreted in various ways to suit the individual; female athletes of color have measured success from history and societal expectations. The researcher concluded that athletic success does not come from winning, yet from perceptions and a clear understanding of self.

Recommendations

The research is not completed on this topic. There are more females of color participating in sports than ever before, with the ability to play freely and compete with the best in that sport throughout the world. The ability to compete without cynicism, allowing for other researchers to follow females in sport as it pertains solely to their sexuality. There is more to learn from the boom of technology with sports and also the lack of education for many of the future young ladies.

The new generations seem to be out of touch with legends and the struggle from of old. Creating a historical lesson of culture for females of color through sports can help raise awareness of females of color in sports; constructing future leaders. Media is at the front of perceptions of self and how others view someone. By researching how to use the media, there can be room for positive improvement with females participating in sports.

MIAMI REDHAWKS

2006-07 / 2007-08   Women's Basketball **Roster** a Player:

21 CHANELL RIDLEY

References

Adams, N., Schmitke, A., & Franklin, A. (2005). Tomboys, dykes, and girly girls: Interrogating the subjectivities of adolescent female athletes. Women's Studies Quarterly, 33(1), 17-34. Retrieved from http://search.proquest.com/docview/233648696?accountid=42681

Beamon, K. K. (2008). "Used goods": Former African American college student-athletes' perception of exploitation by division I universities. The Journal of Negro Education, 77(4), 352-364. Retrieved from http://search.proquest.com/docview/222072089?accountid=42681

Beamon, K., & Bell, P. (2006). Academics versus athletics: An examination of the effects of background and socialization on African-American male student-athletes. The Social Science Journal, 43, 393-403.

Berryhill, J. C., & Bee, E. K. (2007). Ethnically diverse college students' psychological sense of community: Do their perceptions of campus racial climate influence it? College Student Affairs Journal, 27(1), 76-93. Retrieved from http://search.proquest.com/docview/224819185?accountid=42681

Bruening, J. E., Pastore, D. L., & Armstrong, K. L. (2008). Factors influencing the sport participation patterns of African American females. The ICHPER-SD Journal of Research in Health, Physical Education, Recreation, Sport & Dance, 3(1), 12-21. Retrieved from http://search.proquest.com/docview/818814048?accountid=42681

Cahn, S. (1993). "From the 'Muscle Moll' to the 'Butch' Ballplayer: Mannishness, Lesbianism, and Homophobia in U.S. Women's Sport." Feminist Studies 19 (2): 343-68.

Cahn, S. (1994). Coming on Strong: Gender and Sexuality in Twentieth-Century Women's Sport. Cambridge, MA: Harvard University Press.

Caudwell, J. (1999). Women's football in the United Kingdom. Journal of Sport and Social Issues, 23, 390–402.

Collins, PH. (1991). Black feminist thought. New York: Routledge &Kegan Paul.

Comeaux, E. (2010). Racial Differences in Faculty Perceptions of Collegiate Student-Athletes' Academic and Post-Undergraduate Achievements. Sociology Of Sport Journal, 27(4), 390-412.

Duke, A. & Greer, J. (August, 2008). Athlete as "model" or athlete as "power"? An analysis of gender stereotypes in photographs of athletic women in magazines. Unpublished paper presented at The Association for Education in Journalism and Mass Communication Annual Convention, Chicago, IL.

Foster, K. M. (2003). Panopticonics: The control and surveillance of black female athletes in a collegiate athletic program. Anthropology and Education Quarterly, 34(3), 300-323. Retrieved from http://search.proquest.com/docview/218125697?accountid=42681

Gill Jr., E. L. (2007, May 31). The Prevalence of Black Females in College Sports: It's Just An Illusion. Diverse: Issues in Higher Education. P. 65.

Griffin, P. (1992). "Changing the Game: Homophobia, Sexism, and Lesbians in Sport." Quest (44): 251-65. Veri, M. 1999. "Homophobic Discourse Surrounding the Female Athlete." Quest (51): 355-68.

Hardin, M. & Gréer, J.D. (2009). The influence of gender-role socialization, media use, and sports participation on perceptions of gender-appropriate sports. Journal of Sport Behavior, 32(2), 207-226.

Harrison Jr., L., Sailes, G., Rotich, W. K., & Bimper Jr., A. Y. (2011). Living the dream or awakening from the nightmare: race and athletic identity. Race, Ethnicity & Education, 14(1), 91-103. doi:10.1080/13613324.2011.531982

Harrison, C., & Lampman, B. (2001). The Image of Paul Robeson: Role Model for the Student and Athlete. Rethinking History, 5(1), 117-130. doi:10.1080/13642520010024190

Hawkins, B. (1999). Black student athletes at predominantly White, National Collegiate Athletic Association division I institutions and the pattern of oscillating migrant laborers. Western Journal of Black Studies, 23, 1-9.

Higgenbotham, E. (1992). We were never on a pedestal: Women of color continue to struggle with poverty, racism, and sexism. In M. Anderson &P. Collins (Eds), Race, class and gender, pp. 183-190. Belmont, CA: Wadsworth.

Hurtado, S., Milem, J. F., Clayton-Pedersen, A. R., & Allen, W. R. (1998). Enhancing Campus Climates for Racial/Ethnic Diversity: Educational Policy and Practice. The Review of Higher Education, 21, 279-302.

Jones, A., & Greer, J. (2011). You don't look like an athlete: The effects of feminine appearance on audience perceptions of female athletes and women's sports. Journal of Sport Behavior, 34(4), 358-377. Retrieved from http://search.proquest.com/docview/903979907?accountid=42681

McVee, M. B., Dunsmore, K., & Gavelek, J. R. (2005). Schema theory revisited. Review of Educational Research, 75(4), 531-566.

Meggysey, D. (2000). Athletes in big-time college sport. Society, 37, 24-29.Person, D., Benson-Quaziena, M., & Rogers, A. (2001). Female student athletes and student athletes of color. New Direction for Student Services, 93, 55-64.

Murphy, A. J. (2005). Life Stories of Black Male and Female Professionals: An Inquiry into the Salience of Race and Sports. Journal Of Men's Studies, 13(3), 313-325.

Perry, T., Steele C., & Hillard, A.(2003) Up from the Parched Earth: Toward a Theory of African American Academic Achievement. In Young, Gifted and Black. Pp.1-108. Boston: Beacon Press.

Person, D. R., Benson-Quaziena, M., & Rogers, A. (2001). Female Student Athletes and Student Athletes of Color. New Directions For Student Services, (93), 55.

Reyna, A. (2011). An Introduction to the Arthur Miller Dialogue on "Sports, Media and Race: The Impact on America." Texas Review Of Entertainment & Sports Law, 12(2), 239-249.

Rowley, S. J., Kurtz-Costes, B., Mistry, R., & Feagans, L. (2007). Social Status as a Predictor of Race and Gender Stereotypes in Late Childhood and Early Adolescence. Social Development, 16(1), 150-168. doi:10.1111/j.1467-9507.2007.00376.x

Smith, Y (1992). Women of color in society and sport. Quest, 228-50.

Smith, Y. R. (1995). Women sports leaders and educators of color--their socialization and achievement. Journal of Physical Education, Recreation & Dance, 66(7), 28-28. Retrieved from http://search.proquest.com/docview/215771260?accountid=42681

Winant, H. (1997). Racial dualism at century's end. In The house that race built: Black Americans, U.S. terrain, edited by W. Lubiano. New York: Pantheon Books.

Winkle-Wagner, R. (2008). Not feminist but strong: Black women's reflections of race and gender in college. Negro Educational Review, 59(3), 181-195,238. Retrieved from http://search.proquest.com/docview/219037693?accountid=42681

2009-10 / 2010-11 WOMEN'S BASKETBALL -- # 32

Appendix A
Female Athletes of Color

Questionnaire Part I

Instructions: This questionnaire is designed to measure people's attitudes about athletic issues. There is no right or wrong answer. Different people have different viewpoints. So, try to be as honest as you can. Beside each statement, circle the number that best describes how you feel. Use the scale below to respond to each statement.

1	2	3	4
Strongly Disagree	Disagree	Agree	Strongly Agree

1. I consider myself an athlete.

    1   2   3   4

2. I have many goals related to sport.

    1   2   3   4

3. Most of my friends are athletes.

    1   2   3   4

4. Sport is the most important part of my life.

    1   2   3   4

5. I spend more time thinking about sports than anything else.

    1   2   3   4

6. I need to participate in sports to feel good about myself.

    1   2   3   4

7. Other people see me mainly as an athlete.

    1   2   3   4

8. I feel bad about myself when I do poorly in sports.

    1   2   3   4

9. Sports are the only important things in my life.

    1   2   3   4

10. I would be very depressed if I were injured and could not compete in sports.

    1   2   3   4

Questionnaire Part II

Each answer pertains to how the athlete is perceives their individual sport and how they may be viewed in their sport:

Key:

1 = Never   2 = Hardly ever   3 = Seldom
4 = Occasionally   5 = Often   6 = Usually
7= Always

____1.   My teammates value my position on the team.

____2.   Due to my position on the team, I am valued and an important part of the team.

____3.   My coach respects my opinions, and I am viewed as a leader on my team.

____4.   My coach will do anything to win, even play players who are not as competitive as I am.

____5.   I am in school because of my sport, and without it I would not be in school.

____6.   There are other people (teammates, coaches, etc.) who look like me within my sport.

____7.   I would tell other females in my position to participate (play) in the sport I am currently playing.

____8.   I am successful because of the sport I play.

___9.   I am careful not to be around individuals who do not participate in sports the way I am participating in sports.

___10. I play my sport because of other females who have played this sport.

<u>Questionnaire Part III</u>

Gender

- ☐ Female

Age

- ☐ 11-13
- ☐ 14-16
- ☐ 17-19
- ☐ 20-22
- ☐ 23-25

Sport Participated in

- ☐ Volleyball
- ☐ Soccer
- ☐ Track
- ☐ Softball
- ☐ Basketball
- ☐ Field Hockey
- ☐ Swimming
- ☐ Gymnastics
- ☐ Cheerleading

Education

- ☐ Less than high school diploma
- ☐ High School Diploma
- ☐ Associate's degree
- ☐ Bachelor's degree
- ☐ Graduate or post-graduate degree

Nationality
- ☐ American Indian
- ☐ Asian/Pacific Islander
- ☐ African-American
- ☐ Hispanic

ABOUT THE AUTHOR

Chanell Ridley currently resides on the southside of Fort Wayne, Indiana. Chanell's work has been seen throughout the entire Midwest and her current occupation is in youth work; with the Boys & Girls Clubs of Greater Fort Wayne. Chanell is a part of a lifelong fellowship entitled the 'Journey' with various other youth workers across the state. This book is the first installment of her business ventures with; Lil Lue's Brews & Books, LLC.

Over the course of her life Chanell has participated in many organizations and countless hours of community service. Chanell has earned her Bachelor's degree from the University of Saint Francis in Social Work and her Master's degree from Indiana Institute of Technology in Organizational Leadership.

Youth/Certificate Programs – WNBA-Her Time To Play Program; 21st Century Community Learning; Drug & Alcohol Education; Behavior Management; Suicide Prevention; Healthy Behaviors; Youth Firesetting Behavior; Bullying & Digital Harm; Vulnerable Populations;

Nonviolent Crisis Intervention; Youth Enrichment/Behavior Prevention Strategies & Services; Mental Health Awareness In Youths; Child & Youth (CYC) Certification

Chanell believes in her community and shows love to all who are living, working, or struggling in Fort Wayne. The goal for Chanell and her family is building families within our neighborhoods while producing generational wealth.